T0083065

JOHN RUTTER

LONDON TOWN

A CHORAL CELEBRATION

FOR MIXED AND CHILDREN'S CHOIRS,
WITH PIANO

1.	Prologue: The Bells of London	3
2.	London Zoo	18
3.	Mind the Gap	21
4.	Lines written in the Tower of London	30
5.	The River's Tale	35
6.	Finale and epilogue	41

London Town was commissioned by Children's International Voices of Enfield, in celebration of the 80th birthday of their founder and conductor June Keyte. It was composed in 2018 for performance by Children's International Voices, together with primary and secondary-school choirs from the Borough of Enfield. Grateful thanks are due to the Enfield Residents Priority Fund for their support of the project.

MUSIC DEPARTMENT

OXFORD
UNIVERSITY PRESS

OXFORD
UNIVERSITY PRESS

Great Clarendon Street, Oxford OX2 6DP,
United Kingdom

Oxford University Press is a department of the University of Oxford.
It furthers the University's objective of excellence in research, scholarship,
and education by publishing worldwide. Oxford is a registered trade mark of
Oxford University Press in the UK and in certain other countries

© Collegium Music Publications 2019
Exclusively licensed worldwide to Oxford University Press

John Rutter has asserted his right under the Copyright, Designs
and Patents Act, 1988, to be identified as the Composer of this Work

First published 2019

Impression: 1

All rights reserved. No part of this publication may be reproduced,
stored in a retrieval system, or transmitted, in any form or by any means,
without the prior permission in writing of Oxford University Press

Permission to perform the works in this anthology in public
(except in the course of divine worship) should normally be obtained from
a local performing right licensing organization, unless the owner or the occupier
of the premises being used already holds a licence from such an organization.
Likewise, permission to make and exploit a recording of these works
should be obtained from a local mechanical copyright licensing organization

Enquiries concerning reproduction outside the scope of the above
should be directed to the Music Rights Department, Oxford University Press, at
music.permissions.uk@oup.com or at the address above

ISBN 978–0–19–352838–3

Music originated on Sibelius
Printed in Great Britain on acid-free paper by
Halstan & Co. Ltd, Amersham, Bucks.

LONDON TOWN
A Choral Celebration

JOHN RUTTER

1. Prologue: The Bells of London

(all choirs)

Words by Delphine Chalmers
(Bars 5–23: traditional rhyme)

*The split between younger and older voices is optional – if preferred, all children can sing bars 5–23 throughout, or sopranos and altos from the mixed choir can sing the two portions designated for older children.

© Collegium Music Publications 2019. Exclusively licensed worldwide to Oxford University Press. Text for Nos.1 and 3 © Delphine Chalmers 2019.

OXFORD UNIVERSITY PRESS MUSIC DEPARTMENT, GREAT CLARENDON STREET, OXFORD OX2 6DP
The Moral Rights of the Composer have been asserted. Photocopying this copyright material is ILLEGAL.

17
(*Older voices)
p
can - dle-light; can I get there by can - dle-light? Aye, and back a -
p
22
A Same tempo, ♩.= 72, with a feeling of swinging like bells
- gain.
cresc.
mp
cresc.
28
SOPRANOS
unis.
f
ALTOS
ALL CHOIRS
Perched be-neath the
TENORS
unis.
BASSES
f
mf
cresc.
f
2

33
spire-pricked clouds, We hold the ci-ty's songs. You'll hear us e-cho on the wind:
38
mf
Vi - vos vo - co,
mf
vi - vos
unis.
mp
mor - tu - os plan - go,
mf
mp
mf
Ped.
Ped.
B
43
vo - co,
mp
2
p
mor - tu - os plan - go.
B
2
pp poco a poco cresc.
8vb
2
2
2
2

50
(rhythms need not be exact, random feeling of bells)
C (play as written)
(cresc. sempre)
f
Ped.
56
S.
A.
unis.
f
On the rhyme and chime of our tum - bling peal The
T.
B.
unis.
f
(sim.)
Ped.
(sim.)
60
mf
With fin - gers in - ter - laced, they chase The
bride and groom ap - pear;
mf

64
S.
li - lac pi - geons from the steps In clouds_ of curl-ing con - fet - ti,___ in
A.
li - lac pi - geons from the steps In clouds_ of curl-ing con - fet - ti,___ in
T.
mf
In clouds_ of curl-ing con-
B.
68
clouds_ of curl - ing con - fet - ti.___ The fu - ture sealed with a
clouds_ of curl - ing con - fet - ti.___ The fu - ture sealed with a
-fet - ti,___ The fu - ture sealed with a
mf
In clouds_ of curl - ing con - fet - ti,___ a

71
cresc.
f
kiss, We toll a toast to hap - pi - ness.
76
D
f marcato
On the shrill wag - ging of our clap - per tongues
mf

81
mp
mf
The ci - ty wakes from sleep. Our coarse throats
The ci - ty wakes from sleep. Our coarse throats
The ci - ty wakes from sleep. Our coarse throats
The ci - ty wakes from sleep. Our coarse throats
dim.
mp
mf
85
cresc.
f
hoarse with dust, We sound the a - larm, we sound the a - larm, we
hoarse with dust, We sound the a - larm, we sound the a - larm, we
hoarse with dust, We sound the a - larm, we sound the a - larm,
hoarse with dust, We sound the a - larm, we sound the a - larm,
cresc.
f cresc.
Ped.
Ped.

89
cresc.
ff
E
f
sound the a - larm for fire, war and plague
In - to the star - less
cresc.
ff
f
sound the a - larm for fire, war and plague
In - to the star - less
ff
the a - larm for fire, war and plague
ff
the a - larm for fire, war and plague
E
ff
f
93
mf
dim.
night.
Cus - to - dians of Lon - don's streets, We
mf
dim.
night.
Cus - to - dians of Lon - don's streets, We
f
mf
dim.
In - to the star - less night.
Cus - to - dians of Lon - don's streets, We
mf
dim.
Cus - to - dians of Lon - don's streets, We
dim.
mf
dim.

un poco riten.
a tempo
poco rall.
97
mp
p
keep our stead - fast watch of love.
keep our stead - fast watch of love.
keep our stead - fast watch of love.
keep our stead - fast watch of love.
un poco riten.
a tempo
poco rall.
F A little slower ♩ = 63
102
p lamentoso
On the keen - ing wail of our re - qui - em The black - clad mourn - ers step.
On the keen - ing wail of our re - qui - em The black - clad mourn - ers step.
On the keen - ing wail of our re - qui - em The black - clad mourn - ers step.
On the keen - ing wail of our re - qui - em The black - clad mourn - ers step.
F A little slower ♩ = 63
p lamentoso
r.h.

106
mp
Our wheels grind - ing, turn - ing, we peal full - cir - cle chimes for
mp
Our wheels grind - ing, turn - ing, we peal full - cir - cle chimes for
mp
110
mp
The pro - mise of e - ter - nal rest. Our
mp
The pro - mise of e - ter - nal rest. Our
well - lived lives,
mp
Our
well - lived lives,

114
rip - pling prayers trem - bling soft In the hum of si - lence, si - lence,
p
rall.
dim.
Ped.
118
Slow ♩ = 58
pp
si - lence af - ter sound.
G (♩.= ♩ of previous)
accel.
poco a poco cresc.

123
(accel.)
Tempo I ♩.= 72
mp
cresc.
mf
128
f
H
Our cheeks blush bronze at the
Our cheeks blush bronze at the
Our cheeks blush bronze at the
Our cheeks blush bronze at the
cresc.
f

132
mf
fire-works' flirt - ing, Wel-com-ing New Year. Loose - lipped our voi - ces trip a -
fire-works' flirt - ing, Wel-com-ing New Year. Loose - lipped our voi - ces trip a -
fire-works' flirt - ing, Wel-com-ing New Year. Loose - lipped our voi - ces trip a -
fire-works' flirt - ing, Wel-com-ing New Year.
dim.
mf
137
cresc.
f
-cross the Thames in cla-mour - ing cho - rus, Clang - ing their ca - co - pho - ny,
-cross the Thames in cla-mour - ing cho - rus, Clang - ing their ca - co - pho - ny,
-cross the Thames in cla-mour - ing cho - rus, Clang - ing their ca - co - pho - ny,
Clang - ing their ca - co - pho - ny,
cresc.
f

141
ff
clang - ing their ca - co - pho - ny. Our ma - ny stee - pled
clang - ing their ca - co - pho - ny. Our ma - ny stee - pled
clang - ing their ca - co - pho - ny. Our ma - ny stee - pled
clang - ing their ca - co - pho - ny. Our ma - ny stee - pled
145
I
voi - ces sing: Vi - vos vo - co, mor - tu - os plan - go,
voi - ces sing: Vi - vos vo - co, mor - tu - os plan - go,
voi - ces sing: Vi - vos vo - co, mor - tu - os plan - go,
voi - ces sing: Vi - vos vo - co, mor - tu - os plan - go,

151
mf
dim.
Vi - vos vo - co, mor-tu-os plan - go,
Vi - vos vo - co, mor-tu-os plan - go,
f
vi - vos vo - co, mor-tu-os plan - go, vi - vos vo - co, mor-tu - os plan -
vi - vos vo - co, mor-tu-os plan - go, vi - vos vo - co, mor-tu - os plan -
Ped.
J
159
mp
rall. al fine
p
pp
vi - vos vo - co, vo - co.
-go, mor - tu - os plan - go.
8va

2. London Zoo

(children's choir)

Words by John Rutter

16
mf
The gi - raffes have quite an e - le-gant air, stroll - ing here and there,
mf
20
p
But the e - le-phants car - ry a hea - vy load, They lum - ber a - long on the
p
sim.
24
mf
jun - gle road;
And down in the grass the
mp
Ped.
27
cob - ras crawl, But I real - ly don't like them at all, So I
p
p

30
cresc.
f
run and watch the kan-ga-roos hop, Lick-ing my ice-cream fresh from the shop. I
8va
cresc.
34
wave to the mon-keys and stare at the bears, Feel sad for the pan-da with no one who cares;
f
38
p
cresc.
f
Then I think to my-self rid-ing home on the bus:
dim.
p
cresc.
f
42
cheeky
senza rit.
Do they get bored just look-ing at us?
sfp
sffz

3. Mind the Gap

(*all choirs)

Words by Delphine Chalmers

*Children's choir to join in at conductor's discretion where appropriate.

Text © Delphine Chalmers 2019.

15
Hurt - ling back-wards in our seats, We're tap-ping out a time - hop two - step: Mind the
19
gap and feel the beat, feel the beat, feel the
mp
mp
SOPS and ALTOS
mf
23
beat, feel the beat.
FULL CHOIR
f
cresc.
f
mf
Ped.
27
B SOPS and ALTOS
mf
Ra - cing down the Ju - bi - lee Line To South - wark in six - teen - o -

30
-nine We watch ruffed ac - tors play the round on
elegant
Ped.
33
TENORS and BASSES
mf
long white knu - ckle nights. The Bard may tug his beard in fright But
37
wis - dom will shine through: Our des - ti - ny is in our hands –
41
FULL CHOIR
mp solemn
To thine own self be true.
mp solemn
C TENORS and BASSES
mf
Change here for the
mf

46
FULL CHOIR
mf
North - ern Line For Lon - don Bridge and burn - ing lime. We hear the whip - snap
50
f
SOPS and ALTOS
mf
screech of fire Tear down Pud-ding Lane. The Thames is trem-bling at the
f
mf
legato
54
FULL CHOIR
mf
flames, But Lon - don will be saved: The bu - ckets passed from
58
f
SOPS and ALTOS
mf
hand to hand Prove hard - ship can be braved. So next we're
f
mf

63
D
p
speed-ing down the Ba-ker-loo Line; We reach two-two-one B in time To
p
67
conspiratorial
mf
glimpse the slink - ing sleuth in search of clues in cob-bled lanes; He
tr
f
71
rat - tles off his tight - lipped quips, His an - swer is spot on:
75
(♪ = ♪)
mf TENORS and BASSES
'Al - ways trust your in - stincts – E - le - men - t'ry is
(♪ = ♪)
Ped.

79
poco rall.
FULL CHOIR
mf
E
Slightly broader
♩ = 132
how it's done.'
But when we reach West -
sostenuto
Ped.
83
f
-min-ster In the spring of nine-teen-for-ty - five We see this is a ci - ty That a
f
88
mf
blitz could not de - stroy. One voice of the na - tion Has
mf
Ped.
92
f
brought the coun-try to its feet; We kept the home fires burn - ing Till the
f

96
mp
SOPS and ALTOS
TENORS and BASSES
mp
day when there was peace, there was peace, there was
mp
Ped.
100
rallentando
dim.
FULL CHOIR
p
Tranquillo ♩ = c. 112
F
FULL CHOIR
p legato
peace, there was peace. And as we
dim.
p
Ped.
105
mp
mf
steam in - to King's Cross The en - gine breathes a sigh; We hear the cries of bust - ling por - ters:
mp
mf
Ped.
Ped.
110
mp misterioso
3
Plat - form nine - and - three quar - ters!
8va
mp misterioso
p
Ped.
Ped.

114
rallentando
♩ = 84
G Poco a poco accel.
p
Our words a
(8)
118
cresc.
S.
A.
T.
B.
spell, an in - can - ta - tion, A pro - mise for the fu - ture. We
mf
♪ = ♪
(accel.)
122
Tempo I, fast ♩ = 148
f
ff
plot the map of Lon - don's streets. Mind the

126
mp
cresc.
and feel the beat,
gap
p poco a poco cresc.
129
f
feel the
TENORS
and BASSES
unis.
mf
cresc.
Feel the beat,
f
mf
cresc.
132
cresc.
senza rit.
ff
beat,
feel the beat!
cresc.
ff
senza rit.
f cresc.
ff
8vb

4. Lines written in the Tower of London

(mixed SATB choir only)

Words by Sir Walter Raleigh

9
poco cresc.
mp
youth, our joys, and all we have, And pays us but
poco cresc.
mp
youth, our joys, and all we have, And pays us but
poco cresc.
mp
youth, our joys, and all we have, And pays us but
poco cresc.
mp
youth, our joys, and all we have, And pays us but
poco cresc.
mp
14
dim.
p
with age and dust;
dim.
p
with age and dust;
dim.
p
(p)
with age and dust; Who in the dark and
dim.
p
(p)
with age and dust; Who in the dark and
dim.
p

18
poco rit.
a tempo
p cresc.
When we have
p cresc.
When we have
dim.
pp
si - - lent grave, the dark and si - lent grave,
dim.
pp
si - - lent grave, the dark and si - lent grave, When
poco rit.
a tempo
dim.
pp
p cresc.
22
mf
wan - - - - - dered all our ways,
mf
wan - - - - - dered all our ways,
mf
When we have wan - - - dered all our ways,
mf
we have wan - - - - dered all our ways,
mf

26
mp
dim.
p
Shuts up the sto - ry of our days:
mp
dim.
p
cresc.
Shuts up the sto - ry of our days: And
mp
dim.
p
cresc.
Shuts up the sto - ry of our days: And
mp
dim.
p
Shuts up the sto - ry of our days:
mp
dim.
p
cresc.
30
mp
The Lord shall
(cresc.)
mp
from which earth, and grave, and dust, The Lord shall
(cresc.)
mp
from which earth, and grave, and dust, The Lord shall
(cresc.)
mp
And from which earth, and grave, and dust, The Lord shall
(cresc.)
mp

33
mf
poco rit.
a tempo
rit.
p
raise me up,
I
raise me up,
I
raise me up,
I
raise me up,
I
poco rit.
a tempo
rit.
mf
mp
p
37
a tempo
rall.
trust.
trust.
trust.
trust.
a tempo
rall.
dim.
pp
8vb

5. The River's Tale

(tenors and basses)

Words by Rudyard Kipling (1865–1936)

15
a tempo
mf
"I walk my beat through Lon-don Town, Five hours up and
marcato come prima
20
rit.
p dolce
sev - en down. Up I go till I end my run At Tide-end-town, which is Ted - ding-ton.
legato
p
25
a tempo
mf
f
Down I come with the mud in my hands And plas - ter it o - ver the Map - lin Sands.
mf
f
30
mf
But I'll have you know that these wa - ters of mine Were
mf

35
poco rall.
f
mf
a tempo
once a branch of the Riv - er Rhine, When hun - dreds of miles to the East I went And
39
rit.
a tempo
mf
Eng-land was joined to the Con - ti - nent.
I re- mem - ber the bat - winged
f
mf poco staccato
43
f
liz - ard - birds, the Age of Ice and the mam - moth herds, And the gi - ant ti - gers that
f
47
stalked them down Through Re - gent's Park in - to Cam - den Town.

51
mf
And I re-mem-ber like yes-ter-day The
mf
56
f
ear-liest Cock-ney who came my way, When he pushed through the fo-rest that lined the Strand, With
f
60
p
paint on his face and a club in his hand. He was death to fea-ther and fin and fur. He
p sonore
64
cresc.
mf
cresc.
trapped my bea-vers at West-min-ster. He net-ted my sal-mon, he hunt-ed my deer, He
cresc.
mf
cresc.

68
f
killed my he - ron off Lam - beth Pier.
f
He
f
72
fought his neigh - bour with ax - es and swords, Flint or bronze, at my up - per fords, While
mf
76
mf tranquillo
down at Green - wich, for slaves and tin, The
rall.
mp
sim.
Slow and stately ♩ = 72
mp
tall Phoe - ni - cian ships stole in,
8vb
81
mf
And North Sea war - boats, paint - ed and gay,
a tempo I ♩ = 84
f
Flashed like dra - gon - flies,
mp
mf
E - rith way; And
f
mp
(8)

86
Norse-man and A - rab and Gaul and Greek Drank with the Bri-tons in Bark - ing Creek, And
90
rall.
espress.
(rall. sempre)
f pesante
life was gay, and the world was new, And I was a mile a - cross_ at Kew! But the
espress.
f pesante
94
a tempo ♩ = 84
mf
Ro - man came with a hea - vy hand, And bridged and road-ed and ruled the land, And the
98
rit.
f
a tempo
senza rit.
Ro - man left and the Danes blew in– And that's where your his - to - ry books be - gin!"
mf
f
sffz

6. Finale and epilogue

(*all choirs)

Words: William Wordsworth

*Children sing their designated portions from bar 81 alone, but can also join in elsewhere at conductor's discretion.

11
cresc.
mf
Dull would he be of soul who could pass by a sight so touch - ing in its
15
A
mp
ma - jes - ty: This ci - ty now doth, like a gar - ment, wear the
dim.

19
mf dolce
beau - ty of the morn-ing,
p
the beau - ty of the
mf dolce
beau - ty of the morn-ing,
p
the beau - ty of the
mp
the beau - ty of the morn-ing,
p
the beau - ty of the
mp
the beau - ty of the morn-ing,
p
the beau - ty of the
mp
p
24
poco rit.
morn-ing; si - lent, bare,
B a tempo
cresc.
Ships, tow - ers,
mp cresc.
domes, thea - tres and
morn-ing; si - lent, bare,
cresc.
Ships, tow - ers,
mp cresc.
domes, thea - tres and
morn-ing; si - lent, bare,
p cresc.
tow - ers,
mp cresc.
domes, thea - tres and
morn-ing; si - lent, bare,
mp cresc.
domes, thea - tres and
poco rit.
p
B a tempo
cresc.
Ped.
Ped.
sim.

28
(cresc.)
f
tem - - - ples lie O - pen un - to the fields, and to the
(cresc.)
f
tem - - - ples lie O - pen un - to the fields, and to the
(cresc.)
f
tem - - - ples lie O - pen un - to the fields, and to the
(cresc.)
f
tem - - - ples lie O - pen un - to the fields, and to the
(cresc.)
f
32
mf
sky; All bright and glit - ter - ing in the smoke - less air.
sky;
sky;
sky;
mp delicato

C
36
mp legato espress.
cresc.
mf
Nev - er did sun more beau-ti - ful - ly steep In his first splen- dour, val - ley, rock, or
Nev - er did sun more beau-ti - ful - ly steep In his first splen- dour, val - ley, rock, or
Nev - er did sun more beau-ti - ful - ly steep In his first splen- dour, val - ley, rock, or
Nev - er did sun more beau-ti - ful - ly steep In his first splen- dour, val - ley, rock, or
C
40
p
poco rit.
a tempo
hill; Ne'er saw I, nev - er felt, a calm so deep!
hill; Ne'er saw I, nev - er felt, a calm so deep!
hill; Ne'er saw I, nev - er felt, a calm so deep!
hill; Ne'er saw I, nev - er felt, a calm so deep!
pp

45
D
mp legato
The riv - er gli-deth at his own sweet will:
mp legato
The riv - er gli-deth at his own sweet will:
p
Dear
p
Dear
D
p cresc.
mp
dim.
50
rit.
a tempo
pp
God! the ve - ry hous-es seem a - sleep;
pp
God! the ve - ry hous-es seem a - sleep;
a tempo
rit.
p
dim.
pp
poco a poco cresc.

55
allargando
E a tempo, largamente ♩ = 88
f
Earth has not a - ny-thing to
Earth has not a - ny-thing to
Earth has not a - ny-thing to
Earth has not a - ny-thing to
(cresc.)
allargando
E a tempo, largamente ♩ = 88
60
Tempo I ♩ = 96
mp
cresc.
show more fair: Dull would he be of soul who could
show more fair: Dull would he be of soul who could
show more fair: Dull would he be of soul who could
show more fair: Dull would he be of soul who could
Tempo I ♩ = 96
mp
cresc.

64
poco allarg.
Largamente
mf
f
pass by a sight so touch - ing in its ma - jes - ty: And all that migh - ty
69
poco meno mosso
a tempo I ♩ = 96
p
heart is ly - ing still! And all that migh - ty heart is ly - ing still!

rall.
F Meno mosso ♩.= 72
74
(p)
CHILDREN'S CHOIR
81
mp dreamy
How ma - ny miles to Lon - don town, to Lon - don town, to Lon - don town;
85
how ma - ny miles to Lon - don town? Three - score and ten.
Ped.
90
Can I get there by can - dle-light, by can - dle-light, by can - dle-light; can I get there by

rit.
G ADULT SOPRANOS
p gently
pp
Un poco vivace ♩ = 112
can - dle- light?
Aye, and back a - gain.
ALTOS
TENORS
BASSES
dim.
mf
Ped.
sim.
senza rit.
p cresc.
f cresc.
ff
sffz